SO-ATJ-272

DATE DUE

GAYLORD		PRINTED IN U.S.A.

FIRST AMERICANS

The Arapaho

MICHAEL BURGAN

Marshall Cavendish
Benchmark
New York

ACKNOWLEDGMENTS

Series consultant: Raymond Bial

Marshall Cavendish Benchmark
99 White Plains Road
Tarrytown, New York 10591-5502
www.marshallcavendish.us

Text, maps, and illustrations copyright © 2009 by Marshall Cavendish Corporation
Map by Rodica Prato
Craft illustrations by Chris Santoro
Source for An Arapaho Prayer page 35: http://www.colorado.edu/csilw/arapahoproject/traditional/prayer.htm

Library of Congress Cataloging-in-Publication Data
Burgan, Michael.
The Arapaho / by Michael Burgan.
p. cm. — (First Americans)
Summary: "Provides comprehensive information on the background, lifestyle, beliefs, and present-day lives of the Arapaho people"—Provided by publisher.
Includes bibliographical references and index.
ISBN 978-0-7614-3017-9
1. Arapaho Indians—History—Juvenile literature. 2. Arapaho Indians—Social life and customs—Juvenile literature. I. Title.
E99.A7B87 2009
978.004'97354—dc22
2007033675

Front cover: An Arapaho girl poses during an event on the Wind River Reservation near Riverton, Wyoming.
Title page: A collection of Arapaho stone arrowheads displayed in Thermopolis, Wyoming
Photo research by: Connie Gardner
Cover photo by Raymond Bial
The photographs in this book are used by permission and through the courtesy of: *Nativestock:* Marilyn "Angel" Wynn, 1, 7, 15, 22, 23, 28, 30, 31, 35, 36, 40; *Corbis:* David Muench, 4; William S. Saile, 26; Paul Frenzeny, 33; *Raymond Bial:* 8, 38; *Art Archive:* Gift of William E. Weiss/Buffalo Bill Historical Center, Cody, Wyoming; *NorthWind Picture Archive:* 13, 16, 20, 25; *The Image Works:* Eastcott/Momatiuk, 39.

Editor: Deborah Grahame
Publisher: Michelle Bisson
Art Director: Anahid Hamparian
Series Designer: Symon Chow

Printed in Malaysia
1 3 5 6 4 2

CONTENTS

1 · LIFE ON THE PLAINS

More than one thousand years ago, a people who are today called the Arapaho (Uh-RAP-uh-hoe) lived east of the Missouri River. The tribe hunted, fished, and raised corn. At times the Arapaho moved from one place to another, looking for better hunting grounds.

Several hundred years ago, around 1700, the Arapaho left their traditional homelands because they faced attacks from enemy tribes. The Arapaho settled in the **Great Plains**. This huge region sprawls between the Mississippi River and the Rocky Mountains and stretches from southern Canada to northern Texas. Several major rivers branch through the Great Plains, including the Arkansas, the Missouri, and the Platte. Although this area is mostly flat and covered with tall grass,

The Missouri River, seen here in North Dakota, flows through part of the land that the Arapaho once called home.

it also has rolling hills and some woodland that runs along the riverbanks.

For a time, the Arapaho lived in the northwestern corner of Minnesota. One group then headed into southern Canada, where they lived alongside the Blackfeet, who spoke a related language. In Canada the Arapaho first saw Europeans. These newcomers were traders who had come to Canada to trap or trade for beaver pelts and other furs.

Early in the eighteenth century the Arapaho once again felt threatened by enemy tribes, so they headed southwest, into the heart of the Great Plains. A Plains family usually moved its belongings on a sledlike device called a **travois**. To make a travois, two poles were tied together and the front end was placed across a dog's or horse's back. The other ends of the poles dragged on the ground. Tied between the two poles was a platform or net that held belongings. Sometimes women and girls also carried the tribe's goods on their backs.

On the Great Plains the Arapaho no longer farmed. Instead they moved from one area to another to hunt buffalo and other game. They lived in cone-shaped tents called **tipis**, which could be easily set up and taken down. The most plentiful game that the Arapaho hunted was the buffalo, or bison. At this time the Great Plains were covered with herds of the large, shaggy creatures, which fed on grass. Arapaho families worked together to chase the buffalo herds over cliffs. The fall killed some of the animals. Hunters then killed the

A travois pulled by a horse could carry more household goods than one pulled by a dog.

Some Arapaho eventually moved to this land in Wyoming, where they still live today.

remaining wounded buffalos with bows and arrows or spears. Some Arapaho also built log pens and chased and shouted at the bison, scaring them into the pens. Once trapped inside, the animals were easily killed. At times the Arapaho also ate wild berries and vegetables.

As they adjusted to life on the Plains, the Arapaho began to trade with the Comanche tribe for horses. At times the different tribes of the Great Plains and the Southwest also raided each other to get these valuable animals. With horses the Arapaho could easily track down and kill buffalo. For the Arapaho owning horses was a sign of wealth and power. Some children received their first pony when they were born, and both boys and girls became expert riders by the time they were five years old.

Although the Arapaho traded with other tribes, they sometimes battled them too. Their main enemies included

Artist Frederick Remington was famous for showing scenes from Indian life on the Great Plains, such as this painting of a buffalo kill.

the Pawnee, Ute, and Shoshone. The Arapaho had better relations with the Cheyenne and at times lived close to them. The Pawnee seem to have given the Arapaho the name that we use for them today. It comes from the Pawnee word *tirapahu*, which means "trader." In their own language the Arapaho call themselves *Hinon'eino*—"Our People."

By the early 1800s the Arapaho were completely at home in the Great Plains. They roamed over an area that included parts of what are now South Dakota, Nebraska, Kansas, Colorado, and Wyoming. During this time they began to split into two groups. The Northern Arapaho lived near the North Platte River, in northern Nebraska and Wyoming. The Southern Arapaho lived along the Arkansas River in Kansas. Members of both groups often hunted along the South Platte River in Colorado.

Through the 1820s and 1830s U.S. trappers sometimes came to this region, looking for beaver and other fur-bearing animals. The Arapaho did not rely on beaver fur for clothes, so they mostly left the trappers alone. Starting in the 1840s,

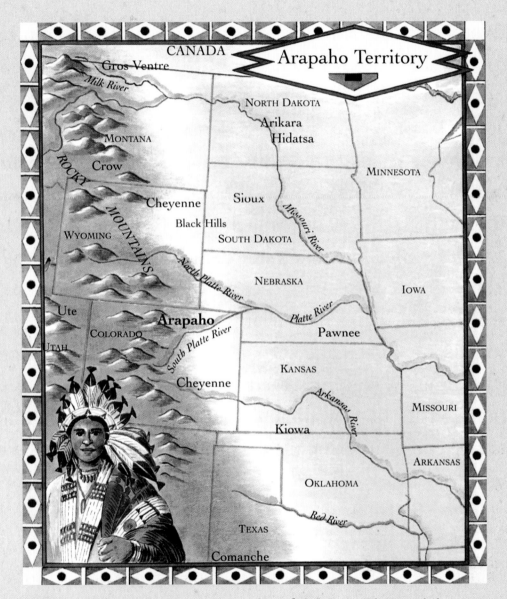

The Arapaho lived on the western edge of the Great Plains, while tribes such as the Sioux and Kiowa lived farther east.

however, the tribe had more contact with settlers, who began to pass through the Great Plains on their way to California and Oregon. The settlers killed buffalo and destroyed the grass that the animals ate to survive. The settlers also spread diseases, such as smallpox, that the Arapaho had never been exposed to before. The new illnesses wiped out thousands of people. By 1850 only three thousand Arapaho lived on the Great Plains, down from ten thousand several decades before. The Arapaho and their **allies** sometimes attacked the settlers, but more still poured west over the Great Plains.

In 1851 the Arapaho joined other neighboring tribes at Fort Laramie, Wyoming. They met to try to improve their relations with the newcomers to their lands. The Arapaho named several chiefs, including Little Owl and Cut Nose, to represent them in talks with the U.S. government officials. The United States agreed to let the tribes hunt on the land where they had hunted for decades, but each tribe had to live in specific areas. The U.S. officials also promised to give the

Indians goods worth $50,000 every year for fifty years. In return the Indians said they would live in peace with each other and U.S. citizens.

Within ten years, however, relations between the Arapaho and Americans soured. In 1858 gold was discovered in the Colorado Rockies, and new settlers flocked to the region. The U.S. government tried to keep the tribes away from the routes the settlers followed. Settlers angered the Arapaho by killing more buffalo. At times the Arapaho starved. They also faced attacks from enemy tribes.

At times, Arapaho and Comanche leaders met to discuss how to fight settlers moving onto their lands.

In November 1864 a group of soldiers attacked a smaller group of Cheyenne and Southern Arapaho living at Sand Creek, Colorado. Between one hundred and two hundred Indians were killed, most of them women, children, and elderly people. The battle is known today as the Sand Creek **Massacre**. A few months later Northern Arapaho warriors joined an Indian force that attacked settlers near the Colorado-Nebraska border. Fighting between newcomers and Great Plains Indians lasted for another twenty-five years. The Arapaho did not take part in most of these early battles. Among the Southern Arapaho, chiefs such as Little Raven and Left Hand urged their people to live peacefully with the settlers. At times, some Northern Arapaho served as scouts for the U.S. Army when the United States was battling other tribes.

In 1867 the Southern Arapaho and Cheyenne agreed to move to a **reservation** in Indian Territory, in what is now Oklahoma and Kansas. Later the reservation was reduced to just part of Oklahoma. For a time some Northern Arapaho also settled on the reservation. In 1878 they were given land at the Wind River Reservation in Wyoming, although they had to share it with their longtime foes, the Shoshone. Chiefs such as Sharp Nose and Black Coal worked with the U.S. government to get food and supplies for the Northern Arapaho.

As buffalo hunters, the Arapaho were used to traveling freely over a wide area. But U.S. officials expected them to farm, wear American-style clothes, and accept Christian religious beliefs. The Arapaho had a hard time adjusting to life on the reservation.

During the Sand Creek Massacre, between eight hundred and one thousand U.S. troops made a surprise attack on the Southern Arapaho and Cheyenne.

2 · LIFE AMONG THE ARAPAHO

The Arapaho believe that everyone goes through the "four hills" of life: childhood, youth, adulthood, and old age. A family's greatest thrill was the arrival of a new baby. Relatives gathered to celebrate what they saw as a gift from the Creator, who had made everything on the earth.

Babies were soon placed in **cradleboards**, wood boards that were covered with hide. The hide formed a pouch to hold the baby. Women decorated the boards with beads and porcupine quills, creating colorful designs. Mothers carried their babies on the boards wherever they went. At times they might hang the board from a nearby tree branch while they collected wild berries or did some other chore.

Arapaho children grew up among related families that formed a camp. The families set up their tipis near each other.

A group of babies are shown sleeping in cradleboards.

Making a Tipi

The simple design of the Arapaho tipi made it easy to set up and take down. The hole in the top let out smoke from campfires, and women carefully opened and closed the side flaps to let in the right amount of air.

You can make your own model of a tipi with these materials:

- A large brown grocery bag, opened at the seams
- One sheet of construction paper
- 4 straight twigs, about 8 inches long
- rubber band or string
- scissors
- paint or markers
- tape

1· Hold the twigs together and place the string or rubber band around them about one inch from the top. Adjust two of the twigs so they form a triangle about two inches wide at the bottom. Trace the triangular shape they form on the construction paper. The top of the triangle should be at the point where the twigs are tied together.

2· Cut out the triangle you drew on the paper, then place it on the opened bag. Trace the triangle on the bag four times. The long edges of the triangles should touch.

3· Cut out this shape along the outside edge. Cut a flap for a door on the bottom edge of one of the triangles. Draw buffalo or designs on what will be the outside of your tipi.

4· Fold the paper along each of the long twig lines. Form the paper into a pyramid or cone shape and tape the outside edges together. Cut off the top of the tipi.

5· Put the twigs inside the tipi. Tape one twig along each fold line.

Your paper tipi is now ready to display—perhaps with others to create an Arapaho village!

From fifteen to twenty buffalo hides were sewn together to create a single tipi.

Families hunted and gathered food together. A number of camps, made up of people with family ties, formed a band. The bands usually only came together a few times a year for large buffalo hunts and religious ceremonies.

Within a family, children called their mother's sister "mother" as well, and her children were called "brothers" and "sisters." A father's brother was also considered a child's father, and his children were brothers and sisters. Each child usually also had a best friend. The friends usually remained close through adulthood.

Children were expected to learn from and obey all the adults around them. Both young boys and girls had their ears pierced, so they would know how to accept pain in life. But Arapaho children were never spanked or hurt in any way.

Children had leisure time, and favorite activities included swimming and playing games. One game involved throwing arrows at targets that were painted on buffalo hide and attached to a rolling hoop. Girls also played with dolls and pretended to be grown women taking care of their families.

As children grew up, boys and girls stopped playing together, and brothers and sisters had less contact with each other. They were expected to stay with the adults of the camp and focus on learning the skills they would need as they grew older. For girls this meant learning how to gather berries and wild plants that were used as food and medicine. Girls also

The Arapaho swapped furs for the colorful glass beads they used to decorate their clothing.

learned how to tan buffalo hides and make clothes from them. Their other tasks included putting up and taking down tipis, gathering firewood, and sewing beads and quills on moccasins and clothing. The women also made **pemmican**, a food made from dried buffalo meat and berries that lasted for months.

Berries, roots, and plant bulbs were part of the Arapaho diet.

With pemmican on hand the Arapaho knew they would not starve if game was scarce.

For boys their lives centered on their future duties as hunters and warriors. From an early age they trained to become expert horse riders. To strengthen their bodies they ran long distances and climbed trees. At times they might also carry dead animals on their backs, so their muscles would

Pemmican

The Arapaho, like other tribes of the Great Plains, used dried buffalo meat to make pemmican. This recipe calls for beef jerky instead, which can be found in most stores. Pemmican can be stored for months without spoiling. It is a popular snack for hikers and campers.

Ask an adult to help you and be careful, because cherry juice can stain clothing.

What You Need:

- 2 cups beef jerky (about 8 ounces)
- 6 tablespoons butter
- 1 cup sour cherries (you can also use dried red cherries, raisins, or other berries)

What You Do:

1. Remove the pits from the cherries and chop them into tiny pieces.
2. Chop the beef jerky in a blender or food processor. Add the cherries.
3. Melt the butter and add to the jerky and cherries. Use a food processor to mix the three ingredients. You can also mix them by hand in a bowl.
4. Shape the mixture into five or six patties.
5. Let the mixture dry in the sun (indoors, near a window) for one or two days.
6. You can also dry the mixture in an oven. Place the patties on a cookie sheet and heat in an oven set at 350 degrees. Cook for about 2 hours, turning the patties over several times.

grow strong. The boys wrestled each other, and they practiced using a bow and arrow. During the 1800s the Arapaho began to trade for firearms, and boys learned to shoot guns as well as use traditional weapons.

Arapaho boys moved through a series of groups called lodges. Arapaho males could join a total of seven lodges throughout their lives. At younger ages they belonged to the first two lodges, Kit Foxes and Stars. They danced and performed other ceremonies out in the open plains. Starting at

A boy and adult worked together to tame wild ponies so they could ride them during hunts and battles.

Powder Face was a Southern
Arapaho war chief of the 1860s.

about the age of ten or twelve, most boys joined the first of the next five lodges that met in tipis inside their own fenced-in areas. Moving through each lodge the Arapaho men sharpened their skills as warriors and learned how to become tribal leaders. The lodges also passed on the unwritten laws of the tribe. The Arapaho did not have books or a written language. All their knowledge about history and religion was passed from one generation to the next through the spoken word. The women had their own lodge, called the Buffalo Lodge, that featured dancing and paid tribute to the most important animal in Arapaho life.

Settlers who met the Arapaho commented on their gentle ways and good sense of humor. When they were forced to fight, however, the Arapaho showed their bravery on the battlefield. Members of the Spear Lodge, usually in their late twenties, were the fiercest Arapaho warriors. Four Spears were chosen to use special clubs, called coup sticks. When a battle started they rushed to the enemy lines on horseback, struck a foe, then tried to return safely to the tribe. This was called **counting coup**. Fighting this way showed the bravery and fighting skills that the Arapaho valued in their warriors.

The next lodge was called the Crazy Lodge. Its members studied the tribe's **rituals** and learned about medicine. Members of the Dog Lodge were older warriors, respected as leaders both on the battlefield and in daily life.

The lodge system began to crumble as the Arapaho moved to reservations, so many younger men never got to be part of the last two lodges. The members of the Sweat Lodge might go along with warriors to a battle, but they usually did not fight. The last lodge was called Seven Old Men. Its members served as priests for the tribe.

The Arapaho believed that people and the world around them came from one source, the Creator. The Arapaho word for the Creator is **Heisonoonin**, and it is sometimes translated as "Man Above" or "Everybody's Father." The Creator gave humans, animals, and other living things a spirit that never died. When the human body died its spirit went to its true home, a distant land above the earth. There it joined the spirits of friends and relatives who had already reached "home."

People could call on the spirits of dead relatives or animals to help protect them from danger. Each person had his or her own prayers, called "medicine," that were used in times of need. People never shared their medicine with others, because that might cause the prayers to lose their power. Some

The Arapaho believed the Creator made everything in the universe, such as these immense clouds over the Arapaho reservation in Wyoming.

Arapaho were said to have medicine that could help them predict the weather, but they also studied the clouds and movement of animals to help with their forecasts.

The Arapaho also had medicine bundles, bags that contained **sacred** objects that could be used to help cure illnesses or help the tribe in war.

A sacred bundle sits in a tree.

The Arapaho believed that Everybody's Father created the Arapaho before he created any other humans. The first Arapaho man had a pipe, which was passed down through the tribe over thousands of years. The Arapaho had special ceremonies to honor this sacred pipe. One man was chosen to be keeper of the pipe. He would carry it and protect it as the tribe moved from place to place. Looking at the pipe was believed to help a person's spirit find its way "home" when the person died. The Arapaho also had a sacred wheel that had forty-eight eagle feathers attached to it. The eagle was said to have special powers for helping the Arapaho. The wheel also had a keeper who watched over it.

Like many tribes the Arapaho had skilled people called **shamans** to lead them in spiritual matters. Shamans also served as doctors. They tried to contact spirits to help cure the sick. The shamans also used herbal teas and roots as medicine. The most important spiritual leaders of the tribe were the members of the Seven Old Men Lodge. These seven priests each had a bag that held powerful medicine that could help the entire tribe.

Each Arapaho man could seek help from the Creator on his own, through a vision quest.

An Arapaho shaman, or "medicine man"

Many Native American tribes use different forms of this spiritual event. In an Arapaho vision quest a man went off by himself for four days. During that time he did not eat. He put all his energy into praying to the Creator. His goal was to contact the spirit world and see something that would give him knowledge. The vision often took the form of an animal. With his new knowledge the Arapaho then returned to the tribe to share what he had learned.

Unlike the vision quest, other Arapaho spiritual events involved groups of people. When a child was born, relatives and elders of the camp held a naming ceremony. The old men and women prayed to the Creator to help the child lead a good life. When a person died, relatives would gather around the grave for four nights and burn cedar leaves. The dead person's spirit was thought to remain with them during this time. The cedar smoke was supposed to keep other spirits away until the dead person's spirit was ready to leave.

The most sacred Arapaho ceremony involved the whole

tribe. Each summer all the bands gathered for the Offerings Lodge, or Sun Dance. This ceremony went on for seven or eight days. The bands set up their tipis in a circle. Following the Arapaho tradition, the opening of each tipi faced the rising sun. Special tipis were erected for the sacred pipe and wheel, and a large circle of poles marked the area where the dancers performed.

Each Sun Dance was sponsored by one member of the tribe and was meant to bring blessings on all the Arapaho.

An Arapaho Prayer

The original Arapaho-language version of this prayer was recorded around 1900 by Alfred Kroeber, a scientist who studied the Arapaho.

Let them hear us, our fathers and our grandfathers
I say this in conjunction with all the heavenly lights;
The yellow day, the good wind,
the good timber, the good earth.
You animals who live below the earth, I pray that you hear my words!
You animals who live on the earth, and in the water, listen to my prayer!
Your surplus is going to be eaten so that the people will prosper,
so that the breath of life will endure for a long time,
so that the tribe will be numerous: the children of all ages,
the girls and boys and men of all ages,
the women and old men, and you old women, of all ages.
(We pray that) these foods will keep us healthy
as long as the sun
follows its path in the sky.
I say to him "my father, listen, and my grandfather,"
the one I am praying to.
(We ask for good) thoughts, a (good) heart, love and a joyful life.
I am now going to share this feast with you, (Man Above).

The dancing at the Offerings Lodge started on the fifth day. Warriors painted their bodies and wore eagle feathers as they danced and prayed for help from the spirit world. They danced near a tree that was cut down and moved to the circle for the ceremony. Also inside the circle was a buffalo skull. By the last day of the dancing, women encouraged the tired men to find the strength to finish.

After the Arapaho moved to the reservations, the U.S. government stopped them from performing the

A buffalo skull, bleached by the sun

Sun Dance. The government wanted to wipe out the tribe's old ways. In recent years, however, the Arapaho have been allowed to hold this sacred ceremony. It takes place on Northern Arapaho lands in Wyoming, and Southern Arapaho travel there to take part in the ceremony.

4 · THE ARAPAHO TODAY

The traditional way of life ended for the Arapaho as they were forced onto reservations. The buffalo hunts were over, and the tribe could no longer ride freely across the Great Plains. For a time some Arapaho still lived in tipis, but in the twentieth century log cabins and other small homes became a common sight on the reservations.

The Northern and Southern Arapaho wrestled with many problems as they tried to adjust to the new ways. Starting in 1892 land that had been set aside for the Southern Arapaho and Cheyenne in Oklahoma was given away to settlers. There and on the Northern Arapaho lands in Wyoming, the people struggled to make a living. Both tribes relied on money from the U.S. government to survive. Over time some Arapaho took jobs off the reservations. The Northern Arapaho

These modern homes are part of the Wind River Reservation in Ethete, Wyoming.

The Northern Arapaho ranch in Wyoming covers 380,000 acres (153,784 hectares) and has more than three hundred horses.

had some success with ranching, and the tribe now raises horses and cattle on Wyoming's largest ranch. Most Southern Arapaho farmed to support themselves. The tribe also earned money from oil that was discovered on their lands. In recent years the Northern Arapaho opened a **casino** to earn money for the tribe.

On the reservations most children were sent away to school. They learned English, and after 1945 few Arapaho children knew how to speak their native language.

Today the reservation at Wind River, Wyoming, has the largest population of Arapaho in the United States. Some 7,400 Arapaho live there, along with 4,200 Eastern Shoshone. At the Oklahoma reservation the Arapaho and Cheyenne now consider themselves one tribe, and about eight thousand

Young Arapaho still learn how to use a bow and arrow, though the equipment is more modern than it was when the tribe lived on the open plains.

During a parade, the Arapaho show pride in both their traditional ways and their ties to the United States.

people belong to it. In both locations the Arapaho are trying to regain some of the culture they lost when they first came to the reservations. Some tribal members live off the reservations in nearby towns.

During the 1980s the Arapaho created their first written alphabet, so they could write down their history and stories. Some tribal elders were recorded speaking Arapaho tales, so the stories would never be forgotten. The tribes now also run their own schools and colleges, so young Arapaho can learn the language their ancestors spoke on the Great Plains.

Spiritual ceremonies are also still important to the Arapaho. The Northern Arapaho still choose a keeper of the sacred pipe and wheel. In 1985 they performed the Paint Ceremony for the first time in almost seventy years. In this ceremony, prayers and face painting are used to remove evil spirits. The Sun Dance also remains a central part of Arapaho life. The Arapaho continue to keep the best from their past, while living in an ever-changing world.

The Spanish bring horses to North America.

The Arapaho settle in the heart of the Great Plains.

The Arapaho begin to split into northern and southern branches.

Settlers traveling west begin to enter Arapaho lands.

The Arapaho join other Great Plains tribes in signing a treaty with the United States.

Gold is discovered in Colorado.

| About 1519 | About 1700 | 1820s | 1840s | 1851 | 1858 |

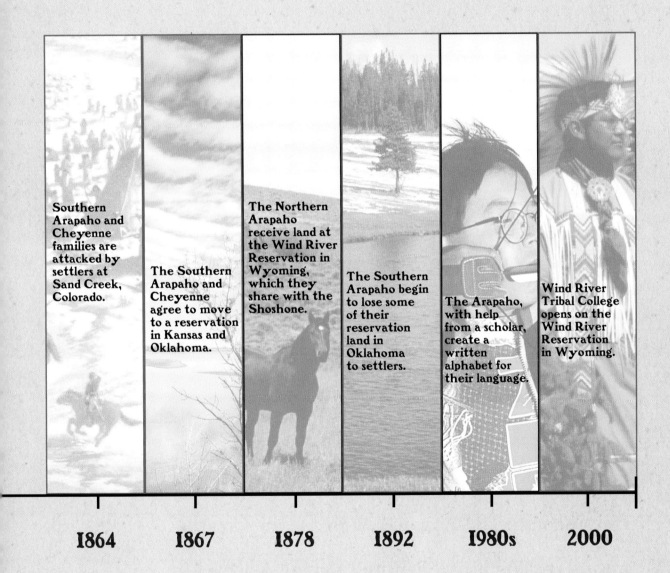

Southern Arapaho and Cheyenne families are attacked by settlers at Sand Creek, Colorado.

The Southern Arapaho and Cheyenne agree to move to a reservation in Kansas and Oklahoma.

The Northern Arapaho receive land at the Wind River Reservation in Wyoming, which they share with the Shoshone.

The Southern Arapaho begin to lose some of their reservation land in Oklahoma to settlers.

The Arapaho, with help from a scholar, create a written alphabet for their language.

Wind River Tribal College opens on the Wind River Reservation in Wyoming.

1864   1867   1878   1892   1980s   2000

· GLOSSARY

allies: People or nations who join together to fight a common enemy.

casino: A place for gambling that also features restaurants and entertainment.

counting coup: Coming close enough to an enemy to touch him with something held in the hand, then getting away unharmed.

cradleboards: Wooden boards partially covered with hide that a mother used to carry her baby.

Great Plains: A huge area of North America that is covered with different kinds of grasses and was once home to massive herds of buffalo.

Heisonoonin: The Arapaho word for the Creator.

massacre: The brutal killing of many defenseless people.

pemmican: Dried meat that is pounded into a powder and mixed with berries and animal fat.

reservation: Land set aside for Native American tribes to live on, after they were forced to leave or gave up their claim to lands where they used to live and hunt.

rituals: Acts performed in a precise way at special ceremonies.

sacred: Holy.

shamans: The healers and spiritual leaders of many Native American tribes.

tipis: The tentlike houses of the Arapaho and other Great Plains tribes. Tipis were made of buffalo hide stretched over poles to create a cone shape. A hole at the top allowed smoke from the fire to escape.

travois: A sledlike device made of two poles tied to the shoulders of a dog or horse and used to carry goods.

• FIND OUT MORE

Books

Broida, Marian. *Projects About the Plains Indians*. New York: Benchmark Books, 2004.

Fowler, Loretta. *The Arapaho*. New York: Chelsea House Publishers, 2006.

Patent, Dorothy Hinshaw. *The Buffalo and the Indian: A Shared Destiny*. New York: Clarion Books, 2006.

Rosinsky, Natalie M. *The Arapaho and Their History*. Minneapolis: Compass Point Books, 2005.

Simmons, Marc. *Friday the Arapaho Boy: A Story from History*. Albuquerque: University of New Mexico Press, 2004.

Web Sites

The Arapaho Project
http://www.colorado.edu/csilw/newarapproj2.htm

Cheyenne and Arapaho Tribes of Oklahoma
http://www.c-a-tribes.org

Northern Arapaho Tribe
http://www.northernarapaho.com

About the Author

Michael Burgan is a former editor at Weekly Reader, where he wrote about current events. As a freelance author, he has written more than 150 books for children and young adults, mostly nonfiction. He is also a playwright. Burgan has a B.A. in history from the University of Connecticut, and currently resides with his wife in Chicago.

· INDEX

Page numbers in **boldface** are illustrations.